Philippe Antonello

✝HE
PASSION

Lessons from the Life of Christ

KEN DUNCAN
PANOGRAPHS®

PHOTOGRAPHS BY KEN DUNCAN & PHILIPPE ANTONELLO
ILLUSTRATIONS BY CHRISTINE FRIEND
DESIGN CONCEPT BY KEN DUNCAN

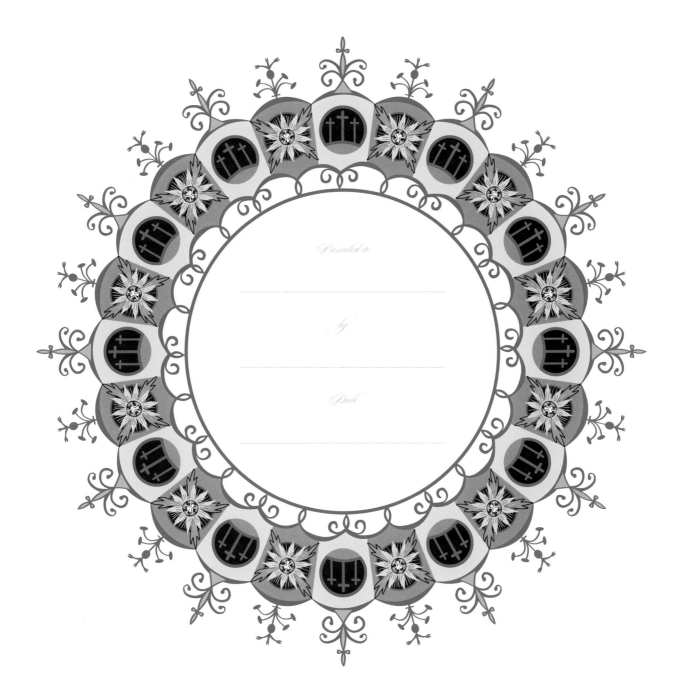

Presented to

_____

by

_____

Date

_____

Jim Caviezel comforts a runaway lamb between takes.

Acknowledgments

I AM THE GOOD SHEPHERD.
THE GOOD SHEPHERD
LAYS DOWN HIS LIFE
FOR THE SHEEP.

John 10:11

This book is dedicated to Jesus who came to pay a debt he didn't owe because we owed a debt we couldn't pay.

Firstly I would like to thank Mel Gibson for having the fortitude to create *The Passion of The Christ* movie and for allowing me to have a small part in this wonderful production by publishing this book. Thanks also to everyone on the movie set, especially Philippe Antonello, for putting up with a landscape photographer who really didn't have a clue what he was up to. A huge thank you to Peter Friend and to my wife, Pamela, for all their assistance in editing the text and to Christine Friend for her beautiful illustrations. Thanks to Tyndale Publishing for the use of their New Living Translation of the Bible for

all scripture quoted. Thanks to Janet Gough – you are a legend – and to my brilliant designer, Peter Morley, for his patience with all the changes. Thanks to all my dedicated staff who persevered with me throughout this epic production. Thanks to Qantas for helping with some airfares along the way. And last, but certainly not least, heartfelt thanks to all those who prayed so diligently throughout the project – you have been a source of great strength to keep me going – especially to my pastors Barry and Lyn Follett. You have all helped tremendously to bring this vision to reality.

Jim Caviezel's script and his precious relics laid out on the Last Supper table.

THE TRUE BREAD OF GOD
IS THE ONE WHO COMES
DOWN FROM HEAVEN
AND GIVES LIFE TO THE WORLD.
...I AM THE BREAD OF LIFE.
NO ONE WHO COMES TO ME
WILL EVER BE HUNGRY AGAIN.

John 0:32-35

This is a movie about love, hope, faith and forgiveness.
He (Jesus) died for all mankind,
suffered for all of us.
It's time to get back to that basic message.
The world has gone nuts.
We could all use a little more love,
hope, faith and forgiveness.

MEL GIBSON

Introduction

When Mel Gibson shared with me his vision for a movie called *The Passion of The Christ* and asked me to take some photographs, I immediately knew I wanted to be part of that project. As I spent time on the movie set, the idea for this book developed.

I felt a divine presence during the production of the movie and was deeply impacted by the power of the story of Christ's suffering as it unfolded before my eyes. Cast and crew members alike were moved to give their utmost during filming. Mel was not concerned about the opinions of his earthly critics, but felt a deep and passionate responsibility to give the film his absolute best to honour his heavenly father. Jim Caviezel also showed incredible dedication to his role and daily spent hours preparing himself spiritually to play the part of Jesus. He carried a few special Christian treasures close to his heart and between takes could often be seen holding these in his hands as he prayed to keep himself centred on the important role he had to play.

In this book I have tried to do more than simply recreate the movie – I have tried to add an extra dimension that will encourage people to see this movie masterpiece for themselves. Hopefully the behind-the-scenes photography, the interviews and the accompanying text will give a greater appreciation of the making of this epic movie. Relevant Bible scriptures are scattered throughout the book in the hope of bringing a deeper insight into the wisdom and divinity of the man called Jesus.

The life of Christ has so greatly impacted the world that time is referenced from His birth. No one has affected the world more than Jesus Christ, so there must be important lessons we can learn from His life. My hope is that you will be drawn into the magic of this movie and that it will touch you as deeply as it has touched me. ✸

Ken Duncan.

Jim Caviezel

FOR GOD SO LOVED THE WORLD
THAT HE GAVE HIS ONLY SON,
SO THAT EVERYONE WHO BELIEVES IN HIM
WILL NOT PERISH BUT HAVE ETERNAL LIFE.

John 3:16

Contents

THE PASSION – LESSONS FROM THE LIFE OF CHRIST

ACKNOWLEDGMENTS	4
Movie Moments	6
INTRODUCTION *by Ken Duncan*	8
LOVE	12
FORGIVENESS	20
INTERVIEW *with Jim Caviezel*	26
Movie Moments	28
Movie Moments	30
GIVING	32
FEAR	38
FAITH	44
PRAYER	48
Movie Moments	54
Movie Moments	56
Movie Moments	58
MERCY	60
Movie Moments	66
Movie Moments	68
INTERVIEW *with Mel Gibson*	70
FREEDOM	74
JOY	80
Movie Moments	86
Movie Moments	88
PEACE	90
INTERVIEW *with Maia Morgenstern*	94
Movie Moments	96
Movie Moments	98
TRUTH	100
Movie Moments	106
Movie Moments	108
HONOUR	110
INTERVIEW *with Caleb Deschanel*	116
GRACE	118
Movie Moments	122
Movie Moments	124
HOPE	126
INTERVIEW *with Monica Bellucci*	130
Movie Moments	132
Movie Moments	134
Movie Moments	136
HUMILITY	138
WORRY	142
SALVATION	146
THE PASSION STORY	154
BLESSING	172
CREDITS	174

Love

I have loved you even as the Father has loved me. Remain in my love. When you obey me, you remain in my love, just as I obey my Father and remain in his love. I have told you this so that you will be filled with my joy. Yes, your joy will overflow! I command you to love each other in the same way that I love you. And here is how to measure it — the greatest love is shown when people lay down their lives for their friends.

John 15:9-13

Here Jim Caviezel portrays Jesus as a young carpenter joyfully embracing his mother (Maia Morgenstern) who has come out to give him a drink. Shot on the first day of filming, this is a portrait warm with love and affection, a snapshot of family life at its best.

Pilate's wife (played by Claudia Gerini) comforts her husband (Hristo Naumov Shopov) in the midst of his inner turmoil. Caught up with him in the drama of Jesus' trial, she is aware that something far bigger than either of them is taking place. All she can offer is her love and understanding.

Jesus staggers under the great weight of his cross.

I COMMAND YOU TO LOVE EACH OTHER
IN THE SAME WAY THAT I LOVE YOU.
AND HERE IS HOW TO MEASURE IT –
THE GREATEST LOVE IS SHOWN WHEN PEOPLE
LAY DOWN THEIR LIVES FOR THEIR FRIENDS.
YOU ARE MY FRIENDS IF YOU OBEY ME.

John 15:12-14

Mary and the young child Jesus. In years to come Mary will watch helplessly as her son is goaded towards the horrors of the cross. But for now she is free to gently comfort the child who has fallen and hurt himself.

SINCE GOD CHOSE YOU
TO BE THE HOLY PEOPLE WHOM HE LOVES,
YOU MUST CLOTHE YOURSELVES
WITH TENDERHEARTED MERCY, KINDNESS,
HUMILITY, GENTLENESS, AND PATIENCE.

Colossians 3:12

A mother's love for her child.

Forgiveness

As they were eating, Jesus took a loaf of bread and asked God's blessing on it. Then he broke it in pieces and gave it to the disciples, saying, "Take it and eat it, for this is my body." And he took a cup of wine and gave thanks to God for it. He gave it to them and said, "Each of you drink from it, for this is my blood, which seals the covenant between God and his people. It is poured out to forgive the sins of many. Mark my words – I will not drink wine again until the day I drink it new with you in my Father's Kingdom."

Matthew 26:26-29

Jesus was brutally whipped even though he had done nothing to warrant such violent punishment.

BUT IF YOU ARE WILLING TO LISTEN,
I SAY, LOVE YOUR ENEMIES.
DO GOOD TO THOSE WHO HATE YOU.
PRAY FOR THE HAPPINESS OF THOSE
WHO CURSE YOU.
PRAY FOR THOSE WHO HURT YOU.

Luke 0:27-28

This is the turning point in Mary Magdalene's life. Her sins forgiven, she reaches for the hand of Jesus and looks into his eyes.

IF WE SAY WE HAVE NO SIN,
WE ARE ONLY FOOLING OURSELVES
AND REFUSING TO ACCEPT THE TRUTH.
BUT IF WE CONFESS OUR SINS TO HIM,
HE IS FAITHFUL AND JUST TO FORGIVE US
AND TO CLEANSE US FROM EVERY WRONG.

1 John 1:8-9

Interview

WITH JIM CAVIEZEL

y first attempt at interviewing Jim Caviezel was not a resounding success. We had sat down to talk in his trailer with Jim fully made up as the badly wounded Jesus. Only afterwards did I realise I had been so discomfited by the experience that I had forgotten to turn the tape recorder on! So it all had to be done again later – this time in the comfort of Jim's home in California. Here the actor who made a name for himself in The Thin Red Line *and* The Count of Monte Cristo *explained why playing Jesus has been the highlight of his career so far.*

How did you come to be cast in the role of Jesus?
Inexplicably I got a call from Mel Gibson. Now I didn't know Mel Gibson, and I wasn't politicking for the role because no one knew it was happening. But we got together and we were sitting on a park bench and he started describing to me this movie that he wanted to make. At that moment I interrupted him and said, "You want me to play Jesus, don't you." And he said, "Yeah." In that one moment a billion thoughts went through my mind, and I thought of all the pain. But to me it was like a big test. If I'd said no, it would have haunted me forever. I didn't want that, so whatever the suffering was to be I said, "Yes, I will play Jesus." So the next day he calls me up. I'm not used to Mel Gibson calling me at home. He said, "This is Mel," and I said, "Mel who?" I really didn't know who it was. He goes, "Mel Brooks." He's so funny. "I've just called you to see if you really want to play this guy," he said. "You're going to be persecuted. It could destroy your career. This is a real career killer." And I just felt the Holy Spirit inside. I said, "Mel, we're not called to the easy life. This is my cross, and if I don't pick it up then I'm going to be crushed under the weight of it."

What was it like actually playing the part of Jesus?
The whole time I kept praying, "Please God, let me play you. In playing you, let me get out of the way. I talk too much. I am too weak. I am going to make mistakes. I am going to sin." Then I started thinking that maybe I didn't have to try so hard. Maybe instead my prayer should be: "God, why don't you play me? Why don't you step inside me since you made me?"

What impact did your character have on others during the filming?
It is amazing how God is revealed to certain individuals, and I got to see this on the set. Sometimes when I walked out, people would come out and cry, and want to hold my hand. Others would look away and they would be amused and point. I thought, time hasn't changed much, has it.

What do you think the message of the movie really is?
Conversion. It's called *The Passion of The Christ*, but it's really about conversion, about man right now. People are always asking me whether there is a resurrection scene in this film. I reply by saying, "Let me ask you this. Will you not believe by seeing the movie alone that Jesus is God? Certainly in the Gospels there were people who did not see the resurrection, but by His Passion alone they believed that he was truly God.

Now that you have played Jesus, do you feel a responsibility to be a good role model in real life?
Yes – for the rest of my life. I spoke to a priest today and I said, "You are called to be abstinent and chaste." I too will have to be chaste for the rest of my life in the roles I take, and the things I do and represent.

Jim Caviezel, free from the burden of his make-up, chats with fellow actors.

Too many people these days simply say, "I'm not your kids' role model," and then think that gives them free reign to do whatever they want. What they're really saying is, "I don't have to be responsible." And that's as ridiculous as saying "I don't believe in Newton's Law" when you're talking about gravity – the real test is when you take a walk off the Empire State Building. No. Just as there are absolutes in math, so there are moral absolutes.

Do you think this film will have a long-term impact?
What I've always said to Mel is: Don't be concerned about this time period, but generations from now. When this movie is living long past your death and when you are forgotten a thousand years from now, they will be talking about this film because they talk about Jesus Christ still until this day. Always there are those who refuse him. But always there are those that are on the fence who will at least go one way or the other. ✿

A number of people attempt to reach the condemned man.
The infuriated Roman soldiers try to keep the crowd back
and are too distracted to notice this woman stride majestically
        towards Jesus and kneel down before him.
She reaches up with a veil to wipe away some of the blood,
sweat and grime and tries to offer Jesus some wine,
but a brutish Roman soldier knocks the goblet out of her
hand onto the ground.

Right: You can always lean on Jesus.

United in their grief after being told of Jesus' arrest, Jesus' mother and Mary Magdalene offer each other support.

The cross brought together the unlikeliest of companions: Roman soldiers, Jesus' closest friends and Joseph of Arimathea.

Giving

You will always reap what you sow! Those who live only to satisfy their own sinful desires will harvest the consequences of decay and death. But those who live to please the Spirit will harvest everlasting life from the Spirit. So don't get tired of doing what is good. Don't get discouraged and give up, for we will reap a harvest of blessing at the appropriate time.

Galations 6:7-9

Jesus with his disciples at the Last Supper .

BREAD FROM HEAVEN
GIVES ETERNAL LIFE
TO EVERYONE WHO EATS IT.
    I AM THE LIVING BREAD
THAT CAME DOWN OUT OF HEAVEN.
    ANYONE WHO EATS THIS BREAD
    WILL LIVE FOREVER;
THIS BREAD IS MY FLESH,
OFFERED SO THE WORLD MAY LIVE.

John 0:50-51

As Jesus reels under the weight of his cross, Simon of Cyrene reaches down to give him a hand up.

After Jesus has fallen for the fourth time, Seraphia offers him a drink and her veil to wipe his face.

Fear

As evening came, Jesus said to his disciples, "Let's cross to the other side of the lake." He was already in the boat, so they started out, leaving the crowds behind (although other boats followed). But soon a fierce storm arose. High waves began to break into the boat until it was nearly full of water. Jesus was sleeping at the back of the boat with his head on a cushion. Frantically they woke him up, shouting, "Teacher, don't you even care that we are going to drown?" When he woke up, he rebuked the wind and said to the water, "Quiet down!" Suddenly the wind stopped, and there was a great calm. And he asked them, "Why are you so afraid? Do you still not have faith in me?" And they were filled with awe and said among themselves, "Who is this man, that even the wind and waves obey him?"

Mark 4:35-41

As Jesus yielded up his spirit at Golgotha, there was a great earthquake that created havoc in the temple and struck fear into the hearts of Caiaphas and the religious leaders. The veil of the temple was torn in two from top to bottom.

THEN JESUS SHOUTED OUT AGAIN,
AND HE GAVE UP HIS SPIRIT.
AT THAT MOMENT THE CURTAIN IN THE TEMPLE
WAS TORN IN TWO, FROM TOP TO BOTTOM.
THE EARTH SHOOK, ROCKS SPLIT APART...
THE ROMAN OFFICER AND THE OTHER SOLDIERS
AT THE CRUCIFIXION WERE TERRIFIED BY
THE EARTHQUAKE AND ALL THAT HAD HAPPENED.
THEY SAID, "TRULY, THIS WAS THE SON OF GOD!

Matthew 27:50-51, 54

The soldiers gambled for his clothes by throwing dice.

Two others, both criminals, were led out to be executed with him.

ONE OF THE CRIMINALS
HANGING BESIDE HIM SCOFFED,
"SO YOU'RE THE MESSIAH, ARE YOU?
PROVE IT BY SAVING YOURSELF –
AND US, TOO, WHILE YOU'RE AT IT!"
BUT THE OTHER CRIMINAL PROTESTED,
"DON'T YOU FEAR GOD
EVEN WHEN YOU ARE DYING?"

Luke 23:39-40

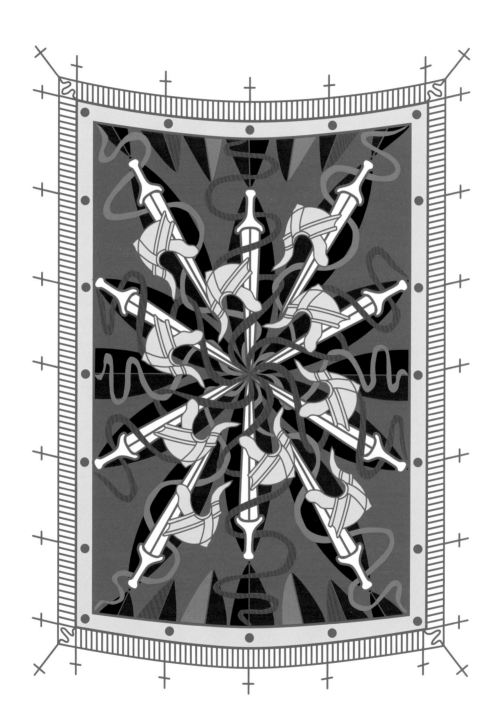

Faith

When Jesus arrived in Capernaum, a Roman officer came and pleaded with him, "Lord, my young servant lies in bed, paralyzed and racked with pain." Jesus said, "I will come and heal him." Then the officer said, "Lord, I am not worthy to have you come into my home. Just say the word from where you are, and my servant will be healed! I know, because I am under the authority of my superior officers and I have authority over my soldiers. I only need to say, 'Go,' and they go, or 'Come,' and they come. And if I say to my slaves, 'Do this or that,' they do it." When Jesus heard this, he was amazed. Turning to the crowd, he said, "I tell you the truth, I haven't seen faith like this in all the land of Israel!"

Matthew 8:5-10

Mel Gibson steps into a shot during one of the most challenging scenes of the film. For Mel, every day on the project was a step of faith. He had put everything on the line – his career, his reputation and many millions of dollars – for a movie he believed must be made.

WHAT IS FAITH?
IT IS THE CONFIDENT ASSURANCE
THAT WHAT WE HOPE FOR
IS GOING TO HAPPEN.
IT IS THE EVIDENCE OF THINGS
WE CANNOT YET SEE.

Hebrews 11:1

Mel's good humour often lightened the mood during scenes that might otherwise have been overwhelming. Here Jesus has been bound in chains in readiness for the judgement before Pilate.

WHENEVER TROUBLE COMES YOUR WAY,
LET IT BE AN OPPORTUNITY
FOR JOY.
FOR WHEN YOUR FAITH IS TESTED,
YOUR ENDURANCE HAS A CHANCE
TO GROW.

James 1:2-3

Prayer

esus said, Pray like this: "Our Father in heaven, may your name be honored. May your Kingdom come soon. May your will be done here on earth, just as it is in heaven. Give us our food for today, and forgive us our sins, just as we have forgiven those who have sinned against us. And don't let us yield to temptation, but deliver us from the evil one."

Matthew 6:9-13

Jesus bows under the weight of the knowledge of his forthcoming trials.

Alone in the agony of his soul, Jesus cries out in prayer in the Garden of Gethsemane.

"FATHER, IF YOU ARE WILLING,
PLEASE TAKE THIS CUP
OF SUFFERING AWAY FROM ME.
YET I WANT YOUR WILL, NOT MINE."
THEN AN ANGEL FROM HEAVEN
APPEARED AND STRENGTHENED HIM.

Luke 22:42-43

Mary Magdalene, played by Monica Bellucci, murmurs a traumatised prayer as Jesus is nailed to the cross. To whom can she turn but God?

Jesus prayed fervently, in such agony of spirit that his sweat fell to the ground like great drops of blood.

An action full of guile. Judas comes to betray Jesus with a kiss.

Judas hangs himself.

WHEN JUDAS, WHO HAD BETRAYED HIM,
REALIZED THAT JESUS HAD BEEN CONDEMNED TO DIE,
HE WAS FILLED WITH REMORSE...
"I HAVE SINNED," HE DECLARED,
"FOR I HAVE BETRAYED AN INNOCENT MAN."

Matthew 27:3-4

Enormous care was taken to ensure the sets
for this movie looked completely authentic.
Here the ancient city of Matera, north of Rome,
is transformed into the marketplace
and streets of Jerusalem,
through which Christ carried his cross.

BECAUSE OF CHRIST
AND OUR FAITH IN HIM,
WE CAN NOW COME FEARLESSLY
INTO GOD'S PRESENCE,
ASSURED OF HIS GLAD WELCOME.

Ephesians 3:12

Anger, raw and unbridled, erupts from the mouth of Caiaphas. Here hatred has overwhelmed reason.

YOUR ANGER
CAN NEVER MAKE THINGS RIGHT
IN GOD'S SIGHT.

James 1:20

The hardness of Rome's professional floggers appears etched in their faces.

DO NOT BRING SORROW
TO GOD'S HOLY SPIRIT
BY THE WAY YOU LIVE.

Ephesians 4:30

Mercy

esus replied with an illustration: "A Jewish man was traveling on a trip from Jerusalem to Jericho, and he was attacked by bandits. They stripped him of his clothes and money, beat him up, and left him half dead beside the road. By chance a Jewish priest came along; but when he saw the man lying there, he crossed to the other side of the road and passed him by. A Temple assistant walked over and looked at him lying there, but he also passed by on the other side. "Then a despised Samaritan came along, and when he saw the man, he felt deep pity.

Kneeling beside him, the Samaritan soothed his wounds with medicine and bandaged them. Then he put the man on his own donkey and took him to an inn, where he took care of him. The next day he handed the innkeeper two pieces of silver and told him to take care of the man. 'If his bill runs higher than that,' he said, 'I'll pay the difference the next time I am here.' "Now which of these three would you say was a neighbor to the man who was attacked by bandits?" Jesus asked. The man replied, "The one who showed him mercy." Then Jesus said, "Yes, now go and do the same."

Luke 10:30-37

This woman showed mercy by wiping Christ's face with her veil and trying to give him a cup of wine.

Jesus takes up his cross again, with the woman clutching the blood-stained veil to her heart.

Simon of Cyrene, enlisted by Roman guards to help carry the cross, here shows compassion for Jesus who has fallen.

Mary, the mother of Jesus, shows tender mercy as she consoles Mary Magdalene in her overwhelming grief.

Mary, the mother of Jesus, and Mary Magdalene have just witnessed a fleeting glimpse of the flagellation of Jesus. In their embrace, they are endeavouring to find some comfort from their despair.

GOD BLESSES THOSE
WHO REALIZE THEIR NEED FOR HIM,
FOR THE KINGDOM OF HEAVEN
IS GIVEN TO THEM.
GOD BLESSES THOSE WHO MOURN,
FOR THEY WILL BE COMFORTED.

Matthew 5:3-4

How would Jesus have prayed?
Mel talks with Jim Caviezel
as they prepare to shoot
the Gethsemane scene.

Philippe Antonello

Mel with the Pharisees.

In the next scene, the crowd will demand that Jesus be crucified.

"By our laws he ought to die," they said,

"because he called himself the Son of God."

Ironically, Mel himself came under considerable religious persecution

for daring to attempt *The Passion of The Christ.*

Some people, it seems, would have preferred

almost any interpretation of the Passion story

except one that tried to be faithful to the original Gospel accounts.

Mary, the mother of Jesus, turned away in horror
as her beloved son was beaten.
Meanwhile, Satan (played by Rosalinda Celentano)
hovered, gloating, with her demonic child
and tried to influence the Roman soldier responsible
for counting the number of lashes Jesus received.
This was an idea introduced by Mel
which brought a surreal quality to the whole scene
as we, the viewers, are the only ones
aware of Satan's presence.

Right: After the flagellation.

Interview

WITH MEL GIBSON

The following is an edited version of an interview I conducted with Mel Gibson in the backlots of Cinecittà film studios, Rome, during filming of The Passion of The Christ. Our discussions took place over a couple of days, chatting over breakfast in Mel's trailer while waiting for the day's scenes to be set up. It was incredible to see Mel directing on set. His passion was contagious. You could see all the actors had great respect for his counsel – they knew that this man was not just a great director but a gifted actor in his own right.

What made you decide to do this movie?
I'd reached a horrible place where I was thinking about jumping out of a window. I wasn't maintaining myself spiritually at all. I believed, but there's a difference between knowing that something exists and actually doing something about it. At that moment I was horrified. I was looking down from twelve floors and seriously thinking I didn't want to stay, but I was too much of a chicken to go splat. So I was stuck in this suspended agony, and it was like I just had to give up. I cried out in prayer, "Help! I need some help here."

Then what happened?
It was strange but things actually got worse for about six months. It was like a trial by fire. But I think you get to a place where, humanly speaking, there's no solution to the Gordian knot that your life has become. So I thought, okay I just have to let what happens happen, and suffer, and hand it all over. And I watched very slowly over the course of six months this thing that had been the most hideous knot drop out into a straight line. I was staggered that my prayer was so effective, because I don't think I had ever really put it into practice, willingly.

Was this when the movie idea was born?
In a way, yes. Because of my experience I started to focus on the Passion of Jesus, which for me, growing up as a kid, had always been sanitised and not real, like a fairytale. It sort of struck me that it really happened, the Word of God tells you that it happened, and it's backed up by every kind of historical detail. So I started to investigate. You know, it's that old thing: "The more you seek, the more you'll find." I was led to certain literature and books, and even medical reports on what must have happened during the Passion. And then I came across the book that this movie is based on. So I read that and was very moved by it.

And what book was that?
The Dolorous Passion of Our Lord Jesus Christ by Anne Catherine Emmerich, a nun in the Eighteenth Century. She was always taking other people's illnesses and she had these visions of the Passion of Christ. All of it completely meshes with the four gospels. It's incredible the minutiae of what she gets into. She tells you about what Jesus was wearing, what the stitching was like. It read like a film script, going from one person to another. It talked in very frank terms about all the people involved, and why they did what they did. Now there's nothing to say that you have to believe this, because it's a vision and it can't be one hundred per cent verified. But in reading you become deeply involved in the emotional aspects, and from your other reading you start cross-referencing in your brain.

How did you begin to translate these ideas into film?
It evolved over a period of ten years. Like most creative things, it started as some half-baked idea

Mel Gibson, Director, on the set of The Passion of The Christ.

then began to take shape over time. (It's not healthy to let these things die. You have to commit it to some art form, otherwise you go nuts.) So I got together with this guy, Ben Fitzgerald. We just started reconstructing the Passion story, cross-referencing with the Biblical accounts. Then we realised we couldn't do that in film. It would take twelve hours. We had to find a way to get the essence of what the book was about, and it had to be short, no longer than ninety minutes, because it's so brutal and so hard. If you stayed in there for two hours and watched this you'd be too wrung out.

What was the response of the major studios when you approached them?
They were interested. I mean, you could tell them you wanted to make a film about cockroach sandwiches and they'd go, "Oh, really?" But they were very guarded too. Hollywood's not a charitable

institution. They don't sit around looking for something good to do. It's a big hard business and it's all about money. So of course this movie looked like a recipe for death to them. Firstly it's on a subject that historically hasn't done well at the box office. Secondly it's in a language that no North American can understand.

So why did you decide to use the ancient languages?
I felt that if we used the language of the day then it would depend on the artistry of the film making process to tell the story. When I researched the languages of the time, I found they spoke Aramaic, Hebrew, Latin and Greek. That was too many languages, so I decided to restrict it to Aramaic and Latin, with the odd bit of Hebrew here and there. The first guy on the project I talked to about it was our writer. "Why do you want to do it like that?" he

said. So I sat him down for about half an hour one day and just talked to him about the effect. He totally got on board. Halfway through the conversation he just got it. He was going, "Oh! Oh! To do it in its own language, it's more powerful that way."

Do you think the risks of doing this movie are worth it?
It's something that is really worth going for and I understand the dangers that are involved with it. Quite frankly, I'm scared because I've never seen a really good version of it. They're always very naïve and put in all the cheating backdrops. It just reeks of falsehood and fairytale. Now we're telling the fact. The fact of the matter is that it was horrible and brutal and we're going to ruffle some feathers. It's going to be violent. I'm sure we're going to cop that one big time – "How dare they do something so irresponsible!" But it's no more violent than a lot of other movies out there and this is a true story.

Do you think this is the most important film you've ever done?
Yes, I think so. It's all been working up to this. It was even in the background when I've made other films, as if they were dry runs for this one.

So do you feel a great responsibility to get this movie right?
Oh absolutely. It's more than great – I feel a grave responsibility. Like I don't want to make even unintentional mistakes. I've been trying to be patient with the stuff that goes slow at times. Like the crucifixion. I couldn't get the whole first third of it, so I thought maybe I wasn't supposed to yet. Maybe I was supposed to figure something out before I got it. But even then I leave every scene thinking I didn't do enough. In some ways, covering with three cameras

drives me absolutely nuts. Watching the dailies, you're watching footage that you know you're never going to use. One scene can last for two hours! But one scene can really only go for a minute to a minute and a half. I'm beating it over the head to make sure I get every possible angle – every opportunity to make each scene as deep and personal as it can possibly be.

Do you think the timing is right for this movie?
I think the timing is too late, but things happen when they are supposed to happen. In fact I was gearing up to do something else. I was supposed to direct *Alexander the Great*, but I got a really hard message – and I mean a really hard message – to drop everything and do this now. I came over to Italy and everything just started falling into place. The producer, Steve McEveety, was amazed. He'd never seen anything fall into place like this from nothing. So there is something quite timely about it. I don't quite understand why.

Do you feel there has been any supernatural intervention?
It's hard to explain, but there have been all sorts of things going on, even down to the small things. Sometimes the weather isn't how you want it, but you set up for the shot anyway and then bingo it just happens. Some really wild stuff too, like with a certain type of dialogue, a big clap of thunder. It's weird. It almost makes you want to laugh. You think, I'll probably have to cut that out because it's too corny! You can only go by your own discernment and taste – from what you've learned over the past twenty-eight years in the film industry.

Ken Duncan

Mel captured between takes in a moment of reflection.

Spiritually and emotionally, how has working on this project affected you?

In a very positive way. Every day we're focusing on the Passion. It begins to inhabit you. At this stage I feel like I'm up to my ears in it, and the effects of it are unavoidable if you do it with the right kind of attitude. There is less ego, and that is a happy by-product. I didn't even realise it was happening until it sort of snuck up on me. I thought, "That's interesting. I'm reacting to things in different ways than I normally would." Many people have offered offences, but because we're doing this I try not letting the little arrows that get fired at me hurt. I don't ignore them, because I know they're there, but I try to understand why they're there and then forgive them, first coldly, then it becomes a habit. What I have achieved is some kind of tranquillity, rather than feeling I have to fight back.

What impact do you hope the movie will have on audiences?

I hope it spurs them on to investigate the life of Christ for themselves. And I don't think you can't be impacted by it. Some of the images are really strong, and I've decided not to hold back. Jim Caviezel said it really well. He said there will be some people that it will freak out. They will give their popcorn back to the earth, like "I'm out of here!" But there will be other people who can't stop watching it, and even though they are horrified and terrified by it they will sit through the whole thing. That's why you only want it to be ninety minutes. You don't want to murder people in there. You want to give them an experience. By speaking very loudly, image and sound wise, it's going to make people think very deeply. ✺

Freedom

Jesus said to the people who believed in him, "You are truly my disciples if you keep obeying my teachings. And you will know the truth, and the truth will set you free."

"But we are descendants of Abraham," they said. "We have never been slaves to anyone on earth. What do you mean, 'set free'?"

Jesus replied, "I assure you that everyone who sins is a slave of sin. A slave is not a permanent member of the family, but a son is part of the family forever. So if the Son sets you free, you will indeed be free."

John 8:31-36

Monica Bellucci enjoys a moment of freedom in the beautiful sunshine during a break between takes.

NOW, THE LORD IS THE SPIRIT,
AND WHEREVER THE SPIRIT OF THE LORD IS,
HE GIVES FREEDOM.

2 Corinthians 3:17

Herod applied his freedom to indulge in a life of debauchery.

Because of his great love for us, Jesus relinquished his freedom.

FOR YOU HAVE BEEN CALLED TO LIVE IN FREEDOM,
NOT FREEDOM TO SATISFY YOUR SINFUL NATURE,
BUT FREEDOM TO SERVE ONE ANOTHER IN LOVE.

Galatians 5:13

Joy

hat night some shepherds were in the fields outside the village, guarding their flocks of sheep. Suddenly, an angel of the Lord appeared among them, and the radiance of the Lord's glory surrounded them. They were terribly frightened, but the angel reassured them. "Don't be afraid!" he said. "I bring you good news of great joy for everyone! The Savior – yes, the Messiah, the Lord – has been born tonight in Bethlehem, the city of David! And this is how you will recognize him: You will find a baby lying in a manger, wrapped snugly in strips of cloth!" Suddenly, the angel was joined by a vast host of others – the armies of heaven – praising God: "Glory to God in the highest heaven, and peace on earth to all whom God favors."

Luke 2:8-14

A movie extra relishes a joyful interlude between takes with a frisky little lamb.

JESUS SAID:
"THE TRUTH IS, YOU CAN GO DIRECTLY
TO THE FATHER AND ASK HIM,
AND HE WILL GRANT YOUR REQUEST
BECAUSE YOU USE MY NAME.
YOU HAVEN'T DONE THIS BEFORE.
ASK, USING MY NAME,
AND YOU WILL RECEIVE,
AND YOU WILL HAVE ABUNDANT JOY."

John 16:23-24

A moment of joy before the days of tumult.

Even amidst the horror of the flagellation scenes, moments of joy were found in the camaraderie between director and actor.

Philippe Antonello

Make-up for Jim Caviezel in his role of Jesus took many hours to apply, but there was still time for a comic waltz with one of the make-up artists.

The scene being shot involves a large cast of extras
and organising them can be a lengthy process.
Camera Operator, Roberto De Angelis,
relaxes in his high perch overlooking the city of Matera
as he waits patiently between takes.

Right: Mary Magdalene

Jim Caviezel's make-up is touched up between takes.

Jim Caviezel takes a break.

Left to right – Steve McEveety, Producer; Caleb Deschanel, Director of Photography and Mel Gibson, Director, discussing the execution of the next shot.

Producer, Bruce Davey, chats during a break with Jim Caviezel.
Shooting for this movie commenced in Italy on November 4th 2002 and continued through until March 25th, 2003 with only a short break for Christmas.
It was a marathon effort for all concerned.

Peace

esus replied, "All those who love me will do what I say. My Father will love them, and we will come to them and live with them. Anyone who doesn't love me will not do what I say. And remember, my words are not my own. This message is from the Father who sent me. I am telling you these things now while I am still with you. But when the Father sends the Counselor as my representative – and by the Counselor I mean the Holy Spirit – he will teach you everything and will remind you of everything I myself have told you. I am leaving you with a gift – peace of mind and heart. And the peace I give isn't like the peace the world gives. So don't be troubled or afraid. Remember what I told you: I am going away, but I will come back to you again. If you really love me, you will be very happy for me, because now I can go to the Father, who is greater than I am. I have told you these things before they happen so that you will believe when they do happen."

John 14:23-29

Mary sits tranquilly at table while her young carpenter son works steadily in the background.

GOD BLESSES THOSE
WHOSE HEARTS ARE PURE,
FOR THEY WILL SEE GOD.
GOD BLESSES THOSE
WHO WORK FOR PEACE,
FOR THEY WILL BE CALLED
THE CHILDREN OF GOD.

Matthew 5:8-9

Despite her lurid past, Mary Magdalene was able to find peace in the forgiveness she received through Jesus Christ.

Interview

*M*aia Morgenstern – who played Jesus' mother Mary – is a Romanian-born actress from a Jewish family background. She has made a name for herself on the Bucharest stage and in a variety of European films. My interview with her took place in her trailer on one of those interminable days of waiting between scenes. It was a pleasure to meet such a delightful and down-to-earth lady – an exceptional actress who is likely to be far more widely appreciated following the release of The Passion of The Christ.

How did you feel when you were cast in the role of Mary?
I was deeply happy. I think it was one of the most important moments in my life as an actress, perhaps the most important. Shaila Rubin, the casting director, had seen me in a number of Romanian and international productions. She thought Mel Gibson might be interested in working with me (I think they had watched some pieces from my films together) and finally Mel Gibson invited me to Rome. I arrived one Monday morning, after an opening night with the Romanian National Theatre – the Jewish theatre in Romania where I work. I have to confess it was a big moment for me, full of emotions and stress and hope. But to get the part, it gave sense to my life once more.

How have you found working with Mel Gibson?
Absolutely wonderful! He is so young and full of life, so full of imagination. And he has such an incredible mix of knowledge – he can jump from one subject to another. At the same time he knows how to make a joke, how to make you smile. On set it's not as if we are in church where nobody moves. Everything is alive, so full of flesh, blood and feeling. Once he gave me a red clown's nose for a joke.

It was late at night, almost early in the morning. Everybody was freezing, everybody was tired. We were rehearsing and waiting, and waiting again. Suddenly Mel gave me this red nose, and when Caleb, the cinematographer, asked me to turn, there I was with a red nose! It was very funny. I think we all needed it at that moment, to be able to smile and laugh.

Do you think this movie is very important to Mel?
Oh yes. It is his life. Even when he is ill, you never see him taking time off. He is always there working, never compromising what he is trying to do. Never. And he is a real artist. It's fantastic how he explains things to us when things are not going well. He shows us what to do. You can see that he's a real actor – in his eyes, in his body.

Were there any moments in the film that really affected you.
The moment when Mary says to Jesus, "Son, allow me to die with you." Let me explain by making a comparison with another film called *The Seventh Room*. There I played Edith Stein, a Jewish-born convert to Catholicism who became a Carmelite nun and died in Auschwitz in 1942. My grandfather also died in Auschwitz, and so when we were shooting Edith Stein's last moments it affected me deeply. I didn't want to make a show, but I felt nothing but ashes in me. It wasn't pain or desperation or madness, only the feeling of ashes, as if there was nothing, nothing, nothing left. There were moments like that too when I was playing Mary, moments when it seemed all purpose in life had gone. When you only want to die, to vanish. That's what it's like as Mary, seeing your child dying. What kind of philosophy can help you then? For that one moment it is only

disaster and hell, and you find in yourself nothing to believe in any more.

And after that, there is a hope?
Yes, after a second the hope comes again. There is a purpose in life. We are not simply machines or objects being manipulated and brainwashed. We find in ourselves the meaning of life, the meaning of hope.

What about the scene where you hold Jesus' body at the foot of the cross?
The Pieta, yes. It was a very difficult scene. We had to shoot it at least three times, trying different camera positions and different ideas. I had visited the Vatican several times, and had seen the *Pieta* by Michelangelo. I had seen the face of the mother of Jesus as shown on the *Pieta*. It was above pain, above suffering. It was a sort of sacrifice. It was like, "I understand and I accept it." It is an incredible quiet beauty, the idea of giving a wonderful gift, a death for the life of the world.

Do you feel there is a great purpose for this movie?
Yes. *The Passion of The Christ* speaks about love. About understanding and communication. So often we are deaf towards others. We don't want to open our ears to anyone else. For me this is the meaning of the film: Let's try and open ourselves to other people. It's not about who is good and who is bad, who is guilty and who is not guilty. It's about each of us involving ourselves in somebody else's dream, getting involved in somebody else's life. ✹

Ken Duncan

Maia Morgenstern in her role as Mary.

In the scene about to be filmed,
Jesus will come forward carrying the cross, and fall.
Here Caleb Deschanel, Director of Photography,
is explaining to Jesus the camera angles he is trying for
and what they are looking for in this particular shot.
Although the ground appears to be solid stone,
a special latex and sponge moulding has been created
to cover a section of the stone pavement,
so the actor is not injured when he falls.

Right: Mel Gibson and Jim Caviezel
share their thoughts on how to treat the next scene.

Satan, played by Rosalinda Celentano, haunts the set like an uninvited spectre. No pleasure is to be found in Satan's ghostly presence, only malevolence and deception..

KEEP ALERT AND PRAY.
OTHERWISE TEMPTATION WILL OVERPOWER YOU.
FOR THOUGH THE SPIRIT IS WILLING ENOUGH,
THE BODY IS WEAK!

Matthew 26:41

Truth

esus told him, "I am the way, the truth, and the life. No one can come to the Father except through me. If you had known who I am, then you would have known who my Father is. From now on you know him and have seen him!"

Philip said, "Lord, show us the Father and we will be satisfied."

Jesus replied, "Philip, don't you even yet know who I am, even after all the time I have been with you? Anyone who has seen me has seen the Father! So why are you asking to see him? Don't you believe that I am in the Father and the Father is in me?

The words I say are not my own, but my Father who lives in me does his work through me. Just believe that I am in the Father and the Father is in me. Or at least believe because of what you have seen me do.

"The truth is, anyone who believes in me will do the same works I have done, and even greater works, because I am going to be with the Father. You can ask for anything in my name, and I will do it, because the work of the Son brings glory to the Father. Yes, ask anything in my name, and I will do it!"

John 14:6-14

Pontius Pilate (Hristo Naumov Shopov) has just interrogated Jesus and he is perplexed by this man. What should he do? "What is truth?" he asks his wife (Claudia Gerini). "Do you hear it? Can you tell me how to recognise it when it is spoken?"

PILATE REPLIED, "YOU ARE A KING THEN?"
"YOU SAY THAT I AM A KING, AND YOU ARE RIGHT,"
JESUS SAID. "I WAS BORN FOR THAT PURPOSE.
AND I CAME TO BRING TRUTH TO THE WORLD.
ALL WHO LOVE THE TRUTH
RECOGNIZE THAT WHAT I SAY IS TRUE."

John 18: 37

Though threatened with crucifixion, Jesus did not seek to justify himself but humbly submitted to the will of God.

AND WHEN YOU ARE BROUGHT TO TRIAL
IN THE SYNAGOGUES AND BEFORE RULERS
AND AUTHORITIES,
    DON'T WORRY ABOUT WHAT TO SAY
IN YOUR DEFENSE [JUSTIFYING YOURSELF],
FOR THE HOLY SPIRIT WILL TEACH YOU
    WHAT NEEDS TO BE SAID
    EVEN AS YOU ARE STANDING THERE.

Luke 12:11-12

The leading priests brought many unjust accusations against Jesus.

The cast of *The Passion of The Christ* showed great respect for
Director, Mel Gibson.

They all enjoyed working with him and valued his wisdom
as not only an award-winning director but also a brilliant actor.
He had a knack of working with the actors – sharing his knowledge
and listening to their ideas – that brought out the best in them.
Here Mel gets up close and personal with Jesus and Simon of Cyrene.
Down on the ground and quickly shuffling backwards to stay out of
the shot, he directs the scene while drawing the actors towards him.

THEN JESUS SAID TO THE DISCIPLES,
"IF ANY OF YOU WANTS TO BE MY FOLLOWER,
YOU MUST PUT ASIDE YOUR SELFISH AMBITION,
SHOULDER YOUR CROSS, AND FOLLOW ME.
IF YOU TRY TO KEEP YOUR LIFE FOR YOURSELF,
    YOU WILL LOSE IT.
BUT IF YOU GIVE UP YOUR LIFE FOR ME,
    YOU WILL FIND TRUE LIFE.
    AND HOW DO YOU BENEFIT
IF YOU GAIN THE WHOLE WORLD
BUT LOSE YOUR OWN SOUL IN THE PROCESS?
IS ANYTHING WORTH MORE THAN YOUR SOUL?"

Matthew 16:24-26

Instruments of torture.

Hands of faith.

Honour

For the Father loves the Son and tells him everything he is doing, and the Son will do far greater things than healing this man. You will be astonished at what he does. He will even raise from the dead anyone he wants to, just as the Father does. And the Father leaves all judgment to his Son, so that everyone will honor the Son, just as they honor the Father. But if you refuse to honor the Son, then you are certainly not honoring the Father who sent him. I assure you, those who listen to my message and believe in God who sent me have eternal life. They will never be condemned for their sins, but they have already passed from death into life.

John 5:20-24

Even on the cross Jesus honoured his mother, handing responsibility for her care over to John. His mother and John, in turn, honoured Jesus by simply being there with him in his distress.

HONOR YOUR FATHER AND MOTHER.
LOVE YOUR NEIGHBOR AS YOURSELF.

Matthew 19:10

Who deserves greater honour than Jesus Christ who laid down his life for all who would believe in him. Even after all the suffering and humiliation inflicted upon him, he was able to say, "Father forgive them, for they know not what they do."

JESUS REPLIED, "THE TIME HAS COME FOR
THE SON OF MAN TO ENTER INTO HIS GLORY.
THE TRUTH IS, A KERNEL OF WHEAT
MUST BE PLANTED IN THE SOIL.
UNLESS IT DIES IT WILL BE ALONE –
A SINGLE SEED. BUT ITS DEATH
WILL PRODUCE MANY NEW KERNELS –
A PLENTIFUL HARVEST OF NEW LIVES."

John 12:23-24

Interview

A hectic week of shooting had made it virtually impossible to find time to interview cinematographer Caleb Deschanel, so we arranged instead to get together on our day off. Chatting over coffee in Caleb's beautiful Old City apartment in Rome, I discovered something about the man behind the camera on such films as The Patriot, Fly Away Home and The Passion of The Christ.

How did you first become involved in this project?
I was on location outside Montreal at the time. I got a call from Steve McEveety, and he seemed very interested in talking to me about where I stood on religion. Basically I was brought up as a Quaker, and I've really had nothing to do with Catholicism although my wife is Catholic. I told them what my point of view was and they sent me the script. I read it and was really impacted by it. It was a really powerful story. I'd never really known that much about Jesus, although obviously everyone knows about Christ being nailed to the cross. For me it was a really great excuse to learn more. The other thing for me was realising this was the story that's inspired so much of the Western World's greatest art. That art would be a wonderful source to draw upon as a visual guide for the movie. So I had a really long talk to Mel. He told me how he was going to do the film in Aramaic and Latin. I thought, "This is just far out enough to be really wonderful!" I could appreciate the power of what he was aiming to do, because so many of the films that influenced me early on were foreign language films.

Is it risky doing a movie like this in terms of your own reputation in Hollywood?
I don't know. I always feel that unless I'm taking chances I get bored. I wish all movies were risky. I get tired of seeing things that I find totally predictable, and this is definitely not predictable. Of all the hundreds of crucifixion pictures that I have looked at over the years and in preparation for this movie, not one of them represents the death of Jesus the same way as it is represented in this film. Everything is sanitised in a way, and in this movie the reality is being presented and it is really horrifying.

You're also doing the lighting for the movie. What have you been hoping to achieve?
Mel and I were both attracted to Caravaggio's paintings, and these have influenced certain aspects of the movie, especially the night scenes and the filming of the Last Supper. We were also trying to create the impression of reality, although there is really no such thing as a reality when you are making a movie. You are making choices all the time, the same way artists in the past made their choices about what the Last Supper looked like, or what it looked like with Jesus on the cross.

How have you found working with Mel?
Mel is really brilliant. He has such a clear vision of what he wants to do, though it takes a little while to get into his head. He can't always express it, and you just have to encourage him to get it out. I try to encourage him not to give up, not to settle for anything less than what he really wants. Often it is a process. What if we go wider? What if we move the camera in here? And it doesn't always happen. The process of making movies is ultimately a whole series of compromises of vision, because your mind is so much more capable of imagining things than can often be realised on film.

Ken Duncan

Caleb Deschanel on set of The Passion of The Christ *contemplating camera angles.*

How do you approach the technical side of cinematography?
I try to learn all the technical things – cameras, lenses, lighting, cranes, remote heads – as well as I can so that they never get in the way of what I really want to do. Then what is inside me can come through. Like the other day. We were doing that scene where Jesus draws the line in the sand and Mary Magdalene comes up. It was an amazing moment.
We photographed it and everything, but in the end it was something separate from Mel or me or Monica or anyone else. It became its own thing, with its own quality of emotion.

What has affected you most in this movie?
Jim Caviezel's performance as Jesus, I think. What is amazing is that there are times where he does not have a lot of dialogue. It's all in his body language and facial expressions. There's no vindictiveness. It's fascinating to see a character who is taking everything without judging the people who are doing this to him, and Jim really plays it in a wonderful way.
I think Mel has done a wonderful job. He has found such an extraordinary number of great actors and great faces for the movie.

Who do you think Jesus was?
I am still learning. There is something very powerful about forgiveness – to me that is the most powerful part of the movie. Drawing upon whatever it was within him, Jesus was able to forgive the most heinous abuses. Certainly the world can use a lot more forgiveness now. If this movie inspires people to rethink their values, then I think it's great.

Grace

To illustrate the point further, Jesus told them this story: "A man had two sons. The younger son told his father, 'I want my share of your estate now, instead of waiting until you die.' So his father agreed to divide his wealth between his sons. "A few days later this younger son packed all his belongings and took a trip to a distant land, and there he wasted all his money on wild living. About the time his money ran out, a great famine swept over the land, and he began to starve. He persuaded a local farmer to hire him to feed his pigs. The boy became so hungry that even the pods he was feeding the pigs looked good to him. But no one gave him anything. When he finally came to his senses, he said to himself, 'At home even the hired men have food enough to spare, and here I am, dying of hunger! I will go home to my father and say, "Father, I have sinned against both heaven and you, and I am no longer worthy of being called your son. Please take me on as a hired man."' So he returned home to his father. And while he was still a long distance away, his father saw him coming. Filled with love and compassion, he ran to his son, embraced him, and kissed him. His son said to him, 'Father, I have sinned against both heaven and you, and I am no longer worthy of being called your son.' But his father said to the servants, 'Quick! Bring the finest robe in the house and put it on him. Get a ring for his finger, and sandals for his feet. And kill the calf we have been fattening in the pen. We must celebrate with a feast, for this son of mine was dead and has now returned to life. He was lost, but now he is found.' So the party began."

Luke 15:11-24

The awful moment of crucifixion – God's son like a lamb, slain for the sins of the world. By this one momentous act God showed his love for an undeserving planet.

MAY GRACE AND PEACE BE YOURS
FROM GOD OUR FATHER
AND FROM THE LORD JESUS CHRIST.
HE DIED FOR OUR SINS,
JUST AS GOD OUR FATHER PLANNED,
IN ORDER TO RESCUE US FROM
THIS EVIL WORLD IN WHICH WE LIVE.

Galatians 1:3-4

Nails, cruel and barbarous, pierced Jesus' hands and feet.
Here Mel Gibson's hand, taking the part of the soldier,
makes a poignant cameo appearance.

Addressing some three hundred extras through a megaphone,
Mel here attempts to whip the mob into a fury for the crucifixion scene.
Throughout the project Mel's passion was contagious.
He knew the necessity of having the crowd with him
at every point as he urged them on to give their best performance.

The process of modern moviemaking is often slow and painstaking.
Here a dolly crane helps position a cameraman high in the air,
while a second camera zooms in for a close-up on the ground.
Many different angles and takes are required to complete
a single minute of finished film.

Satan drifts in the background, influencing the hearts of the people in the crowd and working evil wherever possible at the whipping of Christ.

BUT HE WAS WOUNDED
AND CRUSHED FOR OUR SINS.
HE WAS BEATEN
THAT WE MIGHT HAVE PEACE.
HE WAS WHIPPED,
AND WE WERE HEALED!

Isaiah 53: 5

A soldier pierces Jesus' side to be sure he is dead.

Hope

hen the Pharisees called a meeting and discussed plans for killing Jesus. But Jesus knew what they were planning. He left that area, and many people followed him. He healed all the sick among them, but he warned them not to say who he was. This fulfilled the prophecy of Isaiah concerning him: "Look at my Servant, whom I have chosen. He is my Beloved, and I am very pleased with him. I will put my Spirit upon him, and he will proclaim justice to the nations. He will not fight or shout; he will not raise his voice in public. He will not crush those who are weak, or quench the smallest hope, until he brings full justice with his final victory. And his name will be the hope of all the world."

Matthew 12:14-21

In spite of the agonies ahead, this shot from the Last Supper scene shows Jesus looking out at a future full of hope. His ultimate victory is assured.

HE WILL NOT CRUSH THOSE
WHO ARE WEAK,
OR QUENCH THE SMALLEST HOPE,
UNTIL HE BRINGS FULL JUSTICE
WITH HIS FINAL VICTORY.
AND HIS NAME WILL BE THE HOPE
OF ALL THE WORLD.

Matthew 12:20-21

In a moment of hopelessness, a hand reaches out to embolden Mary. Here John encourages the mother of Jesus to come and support her son in his hour of grief.

WITHOUT WAVERING, LET US HOLD TIGHTLY
TO THE HOPE WE SAY WE HAVE,
FOR GOD CAN BE TRUSTED TO KEEP HIS PROMISE.
THINK OF WAYS TO ENCOURAGE ONE ANOTHER
TO OUTBURSTS OF LOVE AND GOOD DEEDS.

Hebrews 10:23-24

Interview

My interview with Monica Bellucci – who played Mary Magdalene – took place one morning in her make-up area while cast and crew waited for the rain to clear. The day before, I had watched her play the scene in which Mary is dramatically rescued by Jesus from the hands of the mob. I had found it a particularly moving scene, one which epitomises the moment when we reach the end of our own abilities and grasp the hand of the only one who can save us.

How did you first become involved in this movie?
I was shooting an Italian film at the time. During a dinner with Maurizio Millenotti, who is the costume designer for *The Passion of The Christ*, we were talking and he told me that he was preparing a movie with Mel Gibson about the Passion of Jesus. I said, "Who is going to play Mary Magdalene?" He said, "I don't know." So I called my agent in Los Angeles and I said I wanted to meet Mel Gibson. We met and he chose me! So it was really strange. It was miraculous that I was able to get in touch with him and become part of this project just by coincidence.

And what was your impression of Mel?
To meet Mel and land the part, it was so fantastic. I love his enthusiasm. He's full of energy – and those eyes, so beautiful, so deep. I felt this man believed so much in this project. It was very courageous, because these days so many people just do commercial things. Very few ever have the courage to do a project like this one – in Latin and Aramaic. I fell in love with the idea of doing a movie where the images are stronger than the words. It was something new. Courageous, strong and difficult.

Who was Mary Magdalene to you?
I like to think she was a sinner not because she was a prostitute but because she was into material things. Maybe she was a prostitute because she liked to have money. I think when Jesus saves her from being stoned it's like he makes her aware of her own worth as a human being. It's like the first time a man looks at her in a different way. It's so beautiful, the moment of forgiveness, when she is so vulnerable. All those men are trying to kill her, and Jesus saves her. It's so magic the way it was shot of course, and the concept of forgiveness in this scene is so incredible because to me this is the philosophy of Christianity. Mary Magdalene loved Jesus because he set her free. And she is there for him from this moment till the end.

Who was Jesus to you?
I think he was an incredible man. Intelligent, human, so in touch with everybody, so humble. I would have loved the chance to meet him. Jesus said such incredible things. Just the idea of forgiveness and compassion. Compassion is one of the most important concepts in Christianity as I see it, because there is a big duality between the good and the evil in each one of us. It's a fight, and we have to understand the same fight is in everyone.

How has it been working with Mel?
Mel has something very special. He has a very good instinct, and this is a really great quality for a director. It is like he feels the situation, he knows if it is wrong or not. He is also a lot of fun, which really helps lighten the mood when covering such a

Monica between takes, concentrates on staying focused on her role.

powerful subject. Yesterday he stepped in to play the part of Jesus because Jim was still in make-up. Only Mel's lower half was visible. I was lying at his feet, reaching up for his hand, gazing into his eyes like I was a slave. I said, "Remember this moment because I don't do this very often with men!" Mel replied, "Don't worry. This is going to be our little secret. I won't say anything to anybody."

What has affected you most?
The lighting, costumes, sets – everything about this movie is so beautiful it is like a Caravaggio painting coming to life. But I have tried not to watch too much yet. I want to see the film finished, with the music and everything. I want to experience it just as the audience will.

Do you think this is an important movie for the world?
Yes, I believe so. I think that everybody did this movie because they felt something special. People have come from everywhere – different cultures and different religions – all working on a movie about love, forgiveness and compassion. This is the way the world should act. It shows people working together to make a beautiful picture with a powerful message. ✺

To save valuable shooting time while Jim Caviezel
was undergoing wardrobe and make-up changes,
Mel stepped in for a cameo role as Jesus in a short scene
in which only his hands and feet were showing.
When they saw the video replay of that scene
and were happy with the results,
Mel and Monica enjoyed a moment of frivolity.

All were swept off their feet when Jesus said, "I am he."

Philippe Antonello

...NOW WITH BLAZING TORCHES,
LANTERNS, AND WEAPONS,
THEY ARRIVED AT THE OLIVE GROVE.
JESUS FULLY REALIZED
ALL THAT WAS GOING TO HAPPEN TO HIM.
STEPPING FORWARD TO MEET THEM, HE ASKED,
"WHOM ARE YOU LOOKING FOR?"
"JESUS OF NAZARETH," THEY REPLIED.
"I AM HE," JESUS SAID.
JUDAS WAS STANDING THERE WITH THEM WHEN
JESUS IDENTIFIED HIMSELF. AND AS HE SAID,
"I AM HE,"
THEY ALL FELL BACKWARD TO THE GROUND!

John 18:3-0

Here we have the meeting of two worlds.

To the left we see crew members scurrying about the movie set

while the director is deep in thought trying to decide

whether there is anything else he needs to film at that point.

To the right, mother Mary (Maia Morgenstern)

and Mary Magdalene (Monica Bellucci)

concentrate on staying in character

in case they are called for another take of the previous scene.

Humility

esus knew that the Father had given him authority over everything and that he had come from God and would return to God. So he got up from the table, took off his robe, wrapped a towel around his waist, and poured water into a basin. Then he began to wash the disciples' feet and to wipe them with the towel he had around him. When he came to Simon Peter, Peter said to him, "Lord, why are you going to wash my feet?" Jesus replied, "You don't understand now why I am doing it; someday you will." "No," Peter protested, "you will never wash my feet!" Jesus replied, "But if I don't wash you, you won't belong to me." Simon Peter exclaimed, "Then wash my hands and head as well, Lord, not just my feet!" Jesus replied, "A person who has bathed all over does not need to wash, except for the feet, to be entirely clean. And you are clean, but that isn't true of everyone here." For Jesus knew who would betray him. That is what he meant when he said, "Not all of you are clean." After washing their feet, he put on his robe again and sat down and asked, "Do you understand what I was doing? You call me 'Teacher' and 'Lord,' and you are right, because it is true. And since I, the Lord and Teacher, have washed your feet, you ought to wash each other's feet. I have given you an example to follow. Do as I have done to you. How true it is that a servant is not greater than the master. Nor are messengers more important than the one who sends them. You know these things—now do them! That is the path of blessing."

John 13:3-17

Jesus humbled himself and washed the feet of his disciples.

JESUS SAID: "THE GREATEST AMONG YOU
MUST BE A SERVANT.
BUT THOSE WHO EXALT THEMSELVES
WILL BE HUMBLED,
AND THOSE WHO HUMBLE THEMSELVES
WILL BE EXALTED."

Matthew 23:11-12

Worry

So I tell you, don't worry about everyday life – whether you have enough food, drink, and clothes. Doesn't life consist of more than food and clothing? Look at the birds. They don't need to plant or harvest or put food in barns because your heavenly Father feeds them. And you are far more valuable to him than they are. Can all your worries add a single moment to your life? Of course not. And why worry about your clothes? Look at the lilies and how they grow. They don't work or make their clothing, yet Solomon in all his glory was not dressed as beautifully as they are. And if God cares so wonderfully for flowers that are here today and gone tomorrow, won't he more surely care for you? You have so little faith! So don't worry about having enough food or drink or clothing. Why be like the pagans who are so deeply concerned about these things? Your heavenly Father already knows all your needs, and he will give you all you need from day to day if you live for him and make the Kingdom of God your primary concern. So don't worry about tomorrow, for tomorrow will bring its own worries. Today's trouble is enough for today.

Matthew 6:25-34

A movie flashback to Jesus' childhood. Mary runs to help her young son.

A mother's anguish.

Jesus falls for the second time.

Salvation

For only I, the Son of Man, have come to earth and will return to heaven again. And as Moses lifted up the bronze snake on a pole in the wilderness, so I, the Son of Man, must be lifted up on a pole, so that everyone who believes in me will have eternal life.

For God so loved the world that he gave his only Son, so that everyone who believes in him will not perish but have eternal life. God did not send his Son into the world to condemn it, but to save it. There is no judgment awaiting those who trust him. But those who do not trust him have already been judged for not believing in the only Son of God.

John 3:13-18

In a moment filled with the deepest symbolism, Jesus shares a cup of wine at the Last Supper.

AFTER SUPPER JESUS SAID:
"THIS WINE IS THE TOKEN
OF GOD'S NEW COVENANT TO SAVE YOU –
AN AGREEMENT SEALED WITH THE BLOOD
I WILL POUR OUT FOR YOU."

Luke 22:20

Holding the bread aloft, Jesus prepares to break the loaf and distribute it to his disciples. Between Jesus' raised arms is the face of Peter.

JESUS TOOK A LOAF OF BREAD;
AND WHEN HE HAD THANKED GOD FOR IT,
HE BROKE IT IN PIECES
AND GAVE IT TO THE DISCIPLES, SAYING,
"THIS IS MY BODY, GIVEN FOR YOU..."

Luke 22:10

Within a day came the profound fulfilment of that which was foreshadowed by the bread and wine.

Jesus is nailed to the cross in preparation for his crucifixion.

SO EVEN THOUGH JESUS WAS GOD'S SON,
HE LEARNED OBEDIENCE
FROM THE THINGS HE SUFFERED.
IN THIS WAY, GOD QUALIFIED HIM
AS A PERFECT HIGH PRIEST,
AND HE BECAME THE SOURCE OF ETERNAL
SALVATION FOR ALL THOSE WHO OBEY HIM.

Hebrews 5:8-9

The death of God's son secured salvation for all those who believe in him.

FOR IF YOU CONFESS WITH YOUR MOUTH
THAT JESUS IS LORD AND BELIEVE IN YOUR HEART
THAT GOD RAISED HIM FROM THE DEAD,
    YOU WILL BE SAVED.
FOR IT IS BY BELIEVING IN YOUR HEART
THAT YOU ARE MADE RIGHT WITH GOD,
    AND IT IS BY CONFESSING WITH YOUR MOUTH
    THAT YOU ARE SAVED.

Romans 10:9-10

The Passion Story

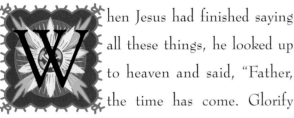

When Jesus had finished saying all these things, he looked up to heaven and said, "Father, the time has come. Glorify your Son so he can give glory back to you. [2]For you have given him authority over everyone in all the earth. He gives eternal life to each one you have given him. [3]And this is the way to have eternal life — to know you, the only true God, and Jesus Christ, the one you sent to earth. [4]I brought glory to you here on earth by doing everything you told me to do. [5]And now, Father, bring me into the glory we shared before the world began.

[6]"I have told these men about you. They were in the world, but then you gave them to me. Actually, they were always yours, and you gave them to me; and they have kept your word. [7]Now they know that everything I have is a gift from you, [8]for I have passed on to them the words you gave me; and they accepted them and know that I came from you, and they believe you sent me.

[9]"My prayer is not for the world, but for those you have given me, because they belong to you. [10]And all of them, since they are mine, belong to you; and you have given them back to me, so they are my glory! [11]Now I am departing the world; I am leaving them behind and coming to you. Holy Father, keep them and care for them — all those you have given me — so that they will be united just as we are. [12]During my time here, I have kept them safe. I guarded them so that not one was lost, except the one headed for destruction, as the Scriptures foretold.

[13]"And now I am coming to you. I have told them many things while I was with them so they would be filled with my joy. [14]I have given them your word. And the world hates them because they do not belong to the world, just as I do not. [15]I'm not asking you to take them out of the world, but to keep them safe from the evil one. [16]They are not part of this world any more than I am. [17]Make them pure and holy by teaching them your words of truth. [18]As you sent me into

the world, I am sending them into the world. [19]And I give myself entirely to you so they also might be entirely yours.

[20]"I am praying not only for these disciples but also for all who will ever believe in me because of their testimony. [21]My prayer for all of them is that they will be one, just as you and I are one, Father – that just as you are in me and I am in you, so they will be in us, and the world will believe you sent me.

[22]"I have given them the glory you gave me, so that they may be one, as we are – [23]I in them and you in me, all being perfected into one. Then the world will know that you sent me and will understand that you love them as much as you love me. [24]Father, I want these whom you've given me to be with me, so they can see my glory. You gave me the glory because you loved me even before the world began!

[25]"O righteous Father, the world doesn't know you, but I do; and these disciples know you sent me. [26]And I have revealed you to them and will keep on revealing you. I will do this so that your love for me may be in them and I in them."

18 Jesus Is Betrayed and Arrested

After saying these things, Jesus crossed the Kidron Valley with his disciples and entered a grove of olive trees. [2]Judas, the betrayer, knew this place, because Jesus had gone there many times with his disciples. [3]The leading priests and Pharisees

Jesus foretells his crucifixion at the Last Supper.

Jesus is betrayed by a kiss from Judas.

Simon Peter cuts the ear off the high priest's servant.

Herod questions Jesus.

As Jesus prays in the Garden of Gethsemane, Satan is seen lurking in the background.

The devil seeks only to steal, kill and destroy. "Deliver us from the evil one," said Jesus in the Lord's Prayer.

Peter's first denial.

Caiaphas questions Jesus.

had given Judas a battalion of Roman soldiers and Temple guards to accompany him. Now with blazing torches, lanterns, and weapons, they arrived at the olive grove.

⁴Jesus fully realized all that was going to happen to him. Stepping forward to meet them, he asked, "Whom are you looking for?"

⁵"Jesus of Nazareth," they replied.

"I am he," Jesus said. Judas was standing there with them when Jesus identified himself. ⁶And as he said, "I am he," they all fell backward to the ground! ⁷Once more he asked them, "Whom are you searching for?"

And again they replied, "Jesus of Nazareth."

⁸"I told you that I am he," Jesus said. "And since I am the one you want, let these others go." ⁹He did this to fulfill his own statement: "I have not lost a single one of those you gave me."

¹⁰Then Simon Peter drew a sword and slashed off the right ear of Malchus, the high priest's servant.¹¹But Jesus said to Peter, "Put your sword back into its sheath. Shall I not drink from the cup the Father has given me?"

Annas Questions Jesus

¹²So the soldiers, their commanding officer, and the Temple guards arrested Jesus and tied him up. ¹³First they took him to Annas, the father-in-law of Caiaphas, the high priest that year. ¹⁴Caiaphas was the one who had told the other Jewish leaders, "Better that one should die for all."

Pilate questions Jesus.

"What is your charge against this man?" asks Pilate.

Peter's First Denial

[15]Simon Peter followed along behind, as did another of the disciples. That other disciple was acquainted with the high priest, so he was allowed to enter the courtyard with Jesus. [16]Peter stood outside the gate. Then the other disciple spoke to the woman watching at the gate, and she let Peter in. [17]The woman asked Peter, "Aren't you one of Jesus' disciples?"

"No," he said, "I am not."

[18]The guards and the household servants were standing around a charcoal fire they had made because it was cold. And Peter stood there with them, warming himself.

The High Priest Questions Jesus

[19]Inside, the high priest began asking Jesus about his followers and what he had been teaching them. [20]Jesus replied, "What I teach is widely known, because I have preached regularly in the synagogues and the Temple. I have been heard by people everywhere, and I teach nothing in private that I have not said in public. [21]Why are you asking me this question? Ask those who heard me. They know what I said."

[22]One of the Temple guards standing there struck Jesus on the face. "Is that the way to answer the high priest?" he demanded.

[23]Jesus replied, "If I said anything wrong, you

Jesus embraces the Cross.

Mary Magdalene, Jesus' mother and John run to comfort Jesus at the cross.

must give evidence for it. Should you hit a man for telling the truth?"

[24]Then Annas bound Jesus and sent him to Caiaphas, the high priest.

Peter's Second and Third Denials

[25]Meanwhile, as Simon Peter was standing by the fire, they asked him again, "Aren't you one of his disciples?"

"I am not," he said.

[26]But one of the household servants of the high priest, a relative of the man whose ear Peter had cut off, asked, "Didn't I see you out there in the olive grove with Jesus?" [27]Again Peter denied it. And immediately a rooster crowed.

Jesus' Trial before Pilate

[28]Jesus' trial before Caiaphas ended in the early hours of the morning. Then he was taken to the headquarters of the Roman governor. His accusers didn't go in themselves because it would defile them, and they wouldn't be allowed to celebrate the Passover feast. [29]So Pilate, the governor, went out to them and asked, "What is your charge against this man?"

[30]"We wouldn't have handed him over to you if he weren't a criminal!" they retorted.

[31]"Then take him away and judge him by your own laws," Pilate told them.

"Only the Romans are permitted to execute someone," the Jewish leaders replied. [32]This fulfilled Jesus' prediction about the way he would die.

[33]Then Pilate went back inside and called for Jesus to be brought to him. "Are you the King of the Jews?" he asked him.

[34]Jesus replied, "Is this your own question, or did others tell you about me?"

[35]"Am I a Jew?" Pilate asked. "Your own people and their leading priests brought you here. Why? What have you done?"

[36]Then Jesus answered, "I am not an earthly king.
If I were, my followers would have fought when I was arrested by the Jewish leaders. But my Kingdom is not of this world."

[37]Pilate replied, "You are a king then?"

"You say that I am a king, and you are right," Jesus said. "I was born for that purpose. And I came to bring truth to the world. All who love the truth recognize that what I say is true."

[38]"What is truth?" Pilate asked. Then he went out again to the people and told them, "He is not guilty of any crime. [39]But you have a custom of asking me to release someone from prison each year at Passover. So if you want me to, I'll

Jesus is led out to be crucified.

John comforts Mary at the foot of the cross.

release the King of the Jews."

⁴⁰But they shouted back, "No! Not this man, but Barabbas!" (Barabbas was a criminal.)

19

Jesus Sentenced to Death

Then Pilate had Jesus flogged with a lead-tipped whip. ²The soldiers made a crown of long, sharp thorns and put it on his head, and they put a royal purple robe on him. ³"Hail! King of the Jews!" they mocked, and they hit him with their fists.

⁴Pilate went outside again and said to the people, "I am going to bring him out to you now, but understand clearly that I find him not guilty." ⁵Then Jesus came out wearing the crown of thorns and the purple robe. And Pilate said, "Here is the man!"

⁶When they saw him, the leading priests and Temple guards began shouting, "Crucify! Crucify!"

"You crucify him," Pilate said. "I find him not guilty."

⁷The Jewish leaders replied, "By our laws he ought to die because he called himself the Son of God."

⁸When Pilate heard this, he was more frightened than ever. ⁹He took Jesus back into the headquarters again and asked him, "Where are you from?" But Jesus gave no answer. ¹⁰"You won't talk to me?" Pilate demanded. "Don't you realize that I have the power to release you or to crucify you?"

¹¹Then Jesus said, "You would have no power over me at all unless it were given to you from above. So the one who brought me to you has the greater sin."

¹²Then Pilate tried to release him, but the Jewish

Jesus on the cross, innocent to the end. The charge above his head read simply: 'Jesus of Nazareth, the King of the Jews.'

The body of Jesus removed from the cross.

leaders told him, "If you release this man, you are not a friend of Caesar. Anyone who declares himself a king is a rebel against Caesar."

[13]When they said this, Pilate brought Jesus out to them again. Then Pilate sat down on the judgment seat on the platform that is called the Stone Pavement (in Hebrew, Gabbatha). [14]It was now about noon of the day of preparation for the Passover. And Pilate said to the people, "Here is your king!"

[15]"Away with him," they yelled. "Away with him – crucify him!"

"What? Crucify your king?" Pilate asked.

"We have no king but Caesar," the leading priests shouted back.

[16]Then Pilate gave Jesus to them to be crucified.

The Crucifixion

So they took Jesus and led him away. [17]Carrying the cross by himself, Jesus went to the place called Skull Hill (in Hebrew, Golgotha). [18]There they crucified him. There were two others crucified with him, one on either side, with Jesus between them. [19]And Pilate posted a sign over him that read, "Jesus of Nazareth, the King of the Jews." [20]The place where Jesus was crucified was near the city; and the sign was written in Hebrew, Latin, and Greek, so that many people could read it.

[21]Then the leading priests said to Pilate, "Change it from 'The King of the Jews' to 'He said, I am King of the Jews.'"

[22]Pilate replied, "What I have written, I have written. It stays exactly as it is."

^{23}When the soldiers had crucified Jesus, they divided his clothes among the four of them. They also took his robe, but it was seamless, woven in one piece from the top. ^{24}So they said, "Let's not tear it but throw dice to see who gets it." This fulfilled the Scripture that says, "They divided my clothes among themselves and threw dice for my robe." So that is what they did.

^{25}Standing near the cross were Jesus' mother, and his mother's sister, Mary (the wife of Clopas), and Mary Magdalene. ^{26}When Jesus saw his mother standing there beside the disciple he loved, he said to her, "Woman, he is your son." ^{27}And he said to this disciple, "She is your mother." And from then on this disciple took her into his home.

The Death of Jesus

^{28}Jesus knew that everything was now finished, and to fulfill the Scriptures he said, "I am thirsty." ^{29}A jar of sour wine was sitting there, so they soaked a sponge in it, put it on a hyssop branch, and held it up to his lips. ^{30}When Jesus had tasted it, he said, "It is finished!" Then he bowed his head and gave up his spirit.

^{31}The Jewish leaders didn't want the victims hanging there the next day, which was the Sabbath (and a very special Sabbath at that, because it was the Passover), so they asked Pilate to hasten their deaths by ordering that their legs be broken. Then their bodies could be taken down. ^{32}So the soldiers came and broke the legs of the two men crucified with Jesus. ^{33}But when they came to Jesus, they saw that he was dead already, so they didn't break his legs. ^{34}One of the soldiers, however, pierced his side with a spear, and blood and water flowed out. ^{35}This report is from an eyewitness giving an accurate account; it is presented so that you also can believe. ^{36}These things happened in fulfillment of the Scriptures that say, "Not one of his bones will be broken," ^{37}and "They will look on him whom they pierced."

The Burial of Jesus

^{38}Afterward Joseph of Arimathea, who had been a secret disciple of Jesus (because he feared the Jewish leaders), asked Pilate for permission to take Jesus' body down. When Pilate gave him permission, he came and took the body away.

Mary Magdalene on her way to the tomb.

The Resurrected Christ.

Philippe Antonello

³⁹Nicodemus, the man who had come to Jesus at night, also came, bringing about seventy-five pounds of embalming ointment made from myrrh and aloes. ⁴⁰Together they wrapped Jesus' body in a long linen cloth with the spices, as is the Jewish custom of burial. ⁴¹The place of crucifixion was near a garden, where there was a new tomb, never used before. ⁴²And so, because it was the day of preparation before the Passover and since the tomb was close at hand, they laid Jesus there.

20 *The Resurrection*

Early Sunday morning, while it was still dark, Mary Magdalene came to the tomb and found that the stone had been rolled away from the entrance. ²She ran and found Simon Peter and the other disciple, the one whom Jesus loved. She said, "They have taken the Lord's body out of the tomb, and I don't know where they have put him!"

³Peter and the other disciple ran to the tomb to see. ⁴The other disciple outran Peter and got there first.

⁵He stooped and looked in and saw the linen cloth lying there, but he didn't go in. ⁶Then Simon Peter arrived and went inside. He also noticed the linen wrappings lying there, ⁷while the cloth that had covered Jesus' head was folded up and lying to the side. ⁸Then the other disciple also went in, and he saw and believed – ⁹for until then they hadn't realized that the Scriptures said he would rise from the dead.

The Roman soldiers were certainly well cast. In their authentic costumes, they presented a fearsome presence on set. Here, their toughness is softened by the warmth of the setting sun while the crew scurry about behind them changing camera angles to try and get in one more shoot for the day.

Blessing

MAY THE LORD BLESS YOU
AND PROTECT YOU.
MAY THE LORD SMILE ON YOU
AND BE GRACIOUS TO YOU.
MAY THE LORD SHOW YOU HIS FAVOR
AND GIVE YOU PEACE.

Numbers 0:24-26

This is the scene where Pontius Pilate asks his wife, "What is Truth?" As Mel talks with them between takes, it almost looks as though he is asking the same question.

The Passion
Lessons from the Life of Christ
First Published and reprinted 2004
by Ken Duncan Panographs® Pty Limited
ABN 21 050 235 606
PO Box 3015, Wamberal NSW 2260
Australia
Telephone +61 2 4367 6777
Email: panos@kenduncan.com

Design concept copyright
© 2004 Ken Duncan
Still photographs taken on film location
by Ken Duncan and Philippe Antonello

All images copyright
© 2004 Icon Distribution, Inc.
All rights reserved.
Illustrations copyright
© 2004 Christine Friend
Designed by Good Catch Design
Reprographics by CFL Print Studio
Printed and bound in China

Scripture quotations are taken from
the Holy Bible, New Living Translation,
copyright © 1996. Used by permission of
Tyndale House Publishers, Inc. Wheaton,
Illinois 60189. All rights reserved.

The National Library of Australia
Cataloguing-in-publication entry:

The Passion: lessons from the life of
Christ: interviews with Mel Gibson, James
Caviezel, Monica Bellucci and others:
images from the movie The Passion of
The Christ.
ISBN 0 9580544 8 7
ISBN 0 9580544 9 5 (Special ed.)
1. Jesus Christ - Passion. 2. Passion of The
Christ (Motion picture). I. Duncan, Ken.
II. Friend, Christine.
232.96

Philippe Antonello

SO KEEP A SHARP LOOKOUT! FOR YOU DO
NOT KNOW WHEN THE LORD WILL RETURN –
AT EVENING, MIDNIGHT, EARLY DAWN, OR
LATE DAYBREAK.
DON'T LET HIM FIND YOU SLEEPING WHEN
HE ARRIVES WITHOUT WARNING.
    WHAT I SAY TO YOU I SAY TO EVERYONE:
WATCH FOR HIS RETURN!"

Mark 13:35-37